DIAGRAMMING —
the key to
understanding grammar

by
Ellen Hajek

BUILDER BOOKS, INC.
P.O. BOX 5789
LYNNWOOD, WA 98046

TABLE OF CONTENTS

Chapter 1 . . .   The Parts of Speech 1

Chapter 2 . . .   Beginning Diagramming--Subjects, Predicates,
                    and Simple Modifiers 12
                         Simple subjects and predicates .   12
                         Adjectives   16
                         Adverbs   18
                         Prepositional Phrases 20

Chapter 3 . . .   Direct Objects and Indirect Objects 26
                         Direct Objects 26
                         Indirect Objects 29

Chapter 4 . . .   Predicate Nouns and Pronouns, Predicate
                    Adjectives 34
                         Predicate nouns and pronouns . .   34
                         Subjective and Objective Forms .   36
                         Using Who and Whom   38
                         Predicate Adjectives   39

Chapter 5 . . .   Compound Modifiers, Compound Subjects and
                         Predicates, Compound Sentences   44
                         Compound Modifiers   44
                         Compound Subjects   46
                         Compound Predicates   48
                         Compound Sentences   50

Chapter 6 . . .   Complex Sentences 56
                         Noun Clauses   56
                         Adjective Clauses   60
                         Adverb Clauses   62

Chapter 7 . . .   Verbals--participles, gerunds, and infinitives 68
                         Participles   68
                         Gerunds   71
                         Infinitives   73

TABLE OF CONTENTS (CONTINUED)

Chapter 8 . . .   Special cases 78
                    Appositive   78
                    Noun of Direct Address 79
                    Parenthetical Material 80

Supplementary Exercises

Answers

CHAPTER ONE
THE PARTS OF SPEECH

Learning to use the English language correctly is somewhat like learning to play a game. Every game comes with a set of rules, and our language has a set of rules, too. We call the rules for using language correctly **grammar**.

If you were learning to play chess, you would soon know that each chess piece has its own special moves. The king, for example, can move only one space in any direction. The queen can move any number of spaces in any direction, and the bishop must move diagonally.

The playing pieces in the English language are called the parts of speech, and each part has a special function.

Identifying the Parts of Speech

NOUN--A *noun* names a person, place, or thing.

> **Example:** *Zeke* hopes to find *gold*.
> "Zeke" and "gold" are both nouns. "Zeke"
> is called a *proper noun* because it is a
> person's name. Proper nouns are capitalized.

> **Exercise:** Complete this sentence by placing
> a noun in the blank.
>
> Zeke will buy ___barbies___ with his gold.

VERB--A *verb* shows action or state of being.

> **Example:** Zeke *shoveled* furiously.

Here the verb is "shoveled," which tells us what Zeke did. "Shoveled" is an action verb.

> **Example:** Now Zeke *is* tired.

Here the verb "is" shows state of being. Zeke is not really doing anything. . . he is just being.

> **Exercise:** Complete this sentence by placing a verb in the blank space.
>
> When Zeke finally saw a bright stone in his pan, he ___yelled___!

Verb (continued)

We use different forms of verbs to show whether
something is in the present, the past, or the future.
We call each of these forms the *tense* of the verb.

Some tenses have a *helping verb* such as **have**,
has, **had**, **shall**, **will**, **is**, **are**, **was**, or **were** with
the main verb.   The verb and the helping verb
are considered as one word.

> **Examples:**
> Present: We *play* softball.
> Past: We *played* softball last week.
> Future: We *shall play* softball next Thursday.
>
> Present Perfect: We *are playing* softball.
> Past Perfect: We *have played* softball every summer.
> Future Perfect: We *shall have played* softball every summer of
> our high school years.

PRONOUN--A *pronoun* substitutes for a noun. It also names a person,
place, or thing, but it is general rather than specific. Some common
pronouns are **he**, **she**, **it**, **they**, **any**, **all**, etc.

Example: He rang the bell.

The pronoun "he" could refer to a boy or to a man or even to an
animal.

Exercise: Complete the following sentence by placing a pronoun in
the blank space.

_She_____ searched for a blue notebook.

Pronouns (continued)

His, **her**, **its**, **their**, **our**, and **my** are pronouns that act as adjectives (described below). They are called *possessive pronouns*.

ADJECTIVE--An *adjective* describes a noun. It tells which one, how many, or what kind. Adjectives often end in -ly, -er, or -est.

Example: Shawna found the *shortest* route.

"Route" is a noun, and "shortest" is an adjective telling us which route.

Example: There were *four* routes.

"Four" is an adjective telling us how many routes there were.

Example: Shawna used the globe during *her* report.

"Her" is a pronoun used as an adjective.

Exercise: Place an adjective in the blank space.

A _____TALL_____ woman entered the room.

ADVERB--An *adverb* describes a verb, an adjective, or another adverb. It tells how, how much, or to what extent. Like adjectives, adverbs often end in -ly. You can tell an adjective from an adverb by finding how the word is used in the sentence.

Example: Lana sang *softly*.

The adverb "softly" describes the verb sang. "Softly" tells us how Lana sang.

Adverbs (continued)

Example: Harding listened *very quietly*.

In this sentence, both "very" and "quietly" are adverbs. "Quietly" tells how Harding listened, and "very" describes the adverb "quietly." Very" tells us to what extent Harding was quiet.

Example: Lana was *unbelievably* talented!

In this sentence, "talented" is an adjective describing the noun Lana, and "unbelievably" is an adverb telling us how talented Lana actually was.

Exercise: Complete the sentence by placing an adverb in the blank space.

Finally, Harding howled ___loudly___ .

PREPOSITION--A *preposition* works with a noun to form a *prepositional phrase*. Prepositions are words such as **on, off, under, around, over, across, beside, of, by, beneath**, etc. that show how the noun in the prepositional phrase relates to the word that the phrase modifies.

Example: Bruno hid *under* the table.

The preposition "under" introduces the phrase "under the table" and relates the noun "table" to the verb "hid."

The prepositional phrase tells us where Bruno hid. The phrase is being used as an adverb describing the verb "hid."

Prepositions (continued)

Exercise: Complete the sentence by placing prepositions in the blank spaces.

A spoon slipped _under_ the table and landed _on_ Bruno.

CONJUNCTION--A conjunction joins two words, phrases, or sentences. There are two types of conjunctions--*coordinating* and *subordinating*. The conjunctions **and, but,** and **or** join words, phrases, or sentences that have equal value. They are called *coordinating* conjunctions.

Example: Mary *and* Kenneth walked to the mailbox.

"And" is a conjunction joining two nouns--"Mary " and "Kenneth."

Example: The old chest lay under a tree *and* near an old well.

"And" joins two prepositional phrases--"under a tree" and "near an old well. "

Example: John wanted to swim, *but* he had no way to get to the pool.

The conjunction "but" joins two complete thoughts--"John wanted to swim" and "He had no way to get to the pool."

Exercise: Complete the sentence by placing a coordinating conjunction in the blank.

Shadow whinnied _and_ stomped.

Conjunction (continued)

The conjunctions **since, because, if, unless, (**and some other words) join thoughts that do not have equal value. One thought depends upon the other to complete its meaning. These conjunctions are known as *subordinating conjunctions.*

Example: *Since* Katharine began taking music lessons, she has not ridden her horse.

The conjunction "since" begins the dependent thought. The words "Since Katharine began taking music lessons" need the rest of the sentence to make sense.

The sentence "She has not ridden her horse" is an independent thought. It makes sense without the rest of the sentence.

Exercise: Complete the sentence by placing a subordinating conjunction in the blank.

Shadow perked up his ears __as_____ he heard Katherine's voice.

INTERJECTION--Interjections are really not part of the structure of a sentence. Interjections are one- or two-word combinations that show strong feeling--surprise, anger, fear, excitement, or joy.

Example: *Ouch*! I burned my finger.

The interjection "ouch" shows surprise.

Exercise: Complete the sentence by placing an interjection in the blank.

_____Wow____! See the fawn!

Using Parts of Speech

Complete the following story by filling in each blank with an appropriate part of speech. You may use words from the lists below or use some of your own choosing.

Nouns--John, child, turtle, Shannon, barn, house.
Verbs--hurried, ran, screamed, rolled, slept, nodded, crept.
Pronouns--he, she, it, her, his, they, theirs.
Adjectives--fast, sharp, loud, angry, old, young.
Adverbs--slowly, very, hardly.
Conjunctions--and, but, or, since.
Prepositions--on, over, off, up.
Interjections--Oh, Look.

The thunder awakened _____John_____. _____He_____
                    1.(proper noun)   2. (pronoun)
turned _____on_____ the light and sat up. I must run
   3. (preposition)
to the _____barn_____ to check on the _____old_____
    4. (noun)   5. (adjective)
_____turtle_____. I must move _____very_____ quickly.
 6.(noun)   7. (adverb)
Just then a streak of lightning flashed, _____and_____ it
                          8. (conjunction)
startled _____John_____.
   9. (noun--same as 1.)

_____Look_____! _____John_____ exclaimed. _____She_____ can't wait!
  10. (interjection)   11. (noun--same as no. 1)   12. (pronoun)

Just for Fun
Name the President

1. I am known as the "father of our country." I am often pictured wearing a white wig. Sometimes I am pictured standing up in a boat!

....

2. They called me "Honest Abe." My home was in a midwestern state.

....

3. I was known as a man of few words. My initials are C.C.

....

4. There were two of us .... (last name). (PLURAL)
   Our first names are T... and
   F...

5. When I retired from the presidency, I began building homes for homeless people. My initials are J.C.

....

Chapter Review

Match each of the items in the left column with the correct item in the right column.

1. VERB

2. PRONOUN

3. ADJECTIVE

4. ADVERB

5. PREPOSITION

6. CONJUNCTION

7. INTERJECTION

8. NOUN

a. is the name of a person, place, or thing.

b. is a word that shows emotion.

c. connects words, phrases, or thoughts.

d. tells when, where, or how.

e. forms a phrase with a noun.

f. tells which one or how many.

g. substitutes for a noun.

h. shows action or state of being

Time to Write

In the column on the left, list three or four special things that you have done that you enjoyed doing. In the column on the right, list three or four things that you would like to do someday. Then, at the bottom of the page, write a few sentences explaining how you will accomplish at least one of the items in the list on your right.

HAVE ALREADY DONE   WANT TO DO

_____   _____

_____   _____

_____   _____

_____   _____

_____

_____

_____

_____

_____

CHAPTER TWO
BEGINNING DIAGRAMMING

Simple Subjects and Predicates

Every sentence has a simple subject and a simple predicate. The simple subject is a noun or pronoun that does something (or has done or will do something or is being something).

> **Example:** The *salesman* talked very fast.

"Salesman" is the subject.

The simple predicate is the verb that tells what the subject is doing (or has done or will do) or is being.

> **Example:** His customer *smiled*.

"Smiled" is the predicate. It tells what the subject did.

We can show how subjects and predicates work together to form sentences with a **diagram**. The simplest form of diagram is that of a simple sentence that has a subject and a predicate. The subject and predicate lie on a straight line with a large vertical line separating them.

Example: SUBJECT | PREDICATE

Simple Subjects and Predicates (continued)

Let's see how this works in a real sentence.

    Example: Fargo meowed.

__Fargo | meowed__

    Notice that in this sentence, "Fargo" is
the subject, and "meowed" is
the predicate.

Now, let's look at another example.

    Example: The bear growled.

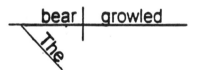

In this sentence, Bear is a noun used as the subject, and growled is a
verb used as the predicate. The article "the" is a little adjective called
an "article. Because "the" refers to the bear, we place it under the
word "bear" in the diagram.

Practice Diagramming

Diagram each of the sentences listed below. Remember to place the subject on the left and the predicate on the right. Place an article under the noun to which it refers.

1. The lion growled.

2. Robby shivered.

3. Sarah cried.

4. The dog whimpered.

5. The movie ended.

More Practice

The sentences below have many more words than the examples you have already seen. Find the simple subject and simple predicate in each sentence and draw a diagram showing only the subject and predicate.

Example: The old lady sat on the bench.

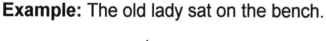

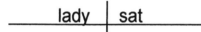

1. The largest dog barked.

2. The light at the top of the hill shone.

3. His little boy played.

4. The cold wind blew yesterday.

5. He shouted at his friend.

Simple Modifiers--Adjectives

An adjective tells something special about the noun it modifies. It may tell which one, how many, or what kind. We often use more than one adjective to describe a noun.

To diagram an adjective, place it on a slanting line under the noun it describes.

Example: The noisy old car smoked.

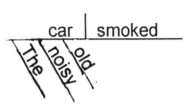

The words "noisy" and "old" are both adjectives. The word "the" is considered to be a small adjective called an *article*.

Let's look at another example.

Example: The fat black cat snarled.

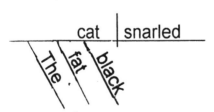

The adjectives in this sentence are "the," "fat," and "black."

Practice Diagramming Adjectives

Find the subject and predicate of each of the following sentences, and place them in a diagram. Then add any adjectives you find to the diagram.

1. The big bug hummed.

2. The tall, dark man sang.

3. The silly old hen clucked.

4. The green parakeet chirped.

5. Harold listened.

Simple Modifiers--Adverbs

Adverbs tell how, how much, to what extent, and where. They describe verbs, adjectives, or other adverbs.

Example: The *most* beautiful girl stood.

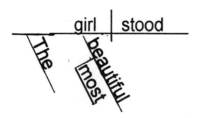

The subject of the sentence is "girl," and the predicate "stood" tells us what "girl" did. "Beautiful" is an adjective describing "girl," and "most" tells us to what extent she is beautiful. "Most" is an adverb.

Example: The audience clapped *loudly.*

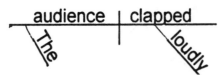

The subject of this sentence is "audience," and the predicate verb is "clapped." "Loudly" tells us how the audience clapped. It is an adverb modifying "clapped."

Example: The audience clapped *very loudly.*

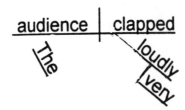

In this sentence, the word "very" tells us about the adverb "loudly." "Very" is an adverb modifying the adverb "loudly."

Practice Diagramming Adverbs

Diagram the following sentences. First place the subject, predicate, and any adjectives you find in the diagram. Then place any adverbs you find.

1. Tina skated gracefully.

2. The brand new skates shone.

3. She turned very sharply.

4. The skates squealed loudly.

5. The very beautiful skater bowed.

Simple Modifiers--Prepositional Phrases

Prepositional phrases are made up of a preposition such as **on**, **about**, **under**, etc. (See the list on p. 5) and a noun or pronoun and sometimes adjectives that describe the noun or pronoun. We call the noun or pronoun following the preposition "the object of the preposition."

Prepositional phrases can act as either adjectives or adverbs. We can diagram prepositional phrases by drawing a line for the phrase and placing a vertical line between the preposition and its object.

Example: The bird *on the bush* sang.

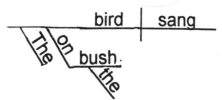

The prepositional phrase "on the bush" is made up of the preposition "on" and followed by the noun "bush." "The" is an article describing "bush." "On the bush" tells which bird sang. The phrase is used as an adjective describing the noun "bird."

Example: The bird sang *on the bush.*

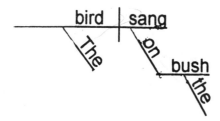

Here the prepositional phrase "on the bush" describes where the bird was when it sang. The phrase is used as an adverb modifying "sang."

Practice Diagramming Prepositional Phrases

Diagram the sentences below by first finding the subject and predicate and putting them into the diagram. Then place adjectives, adverbs, and prepositional phrases.

1. Mark looked into the barrel.

2. The barrel smelled like pine cones.

3. A squirrel watched from a nearby tree.

4. He watched very closely from his perch.

5. Mark grinned at the squirrel.

Possessive Pronouns

Possessive pronouns are pronouns used as adjectives. They refer to a person, place, or thing, but they also describe a noun. Some common possessive pronouns are **my, his**, **her**, **its**, **their**, and **our**.

Possessive pronouns are diagrammed like adjectives.

Example: *His* tail wagged.

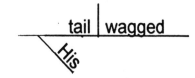

Practice diagramming the following sentences:

1. Her mother called.

2. Its antenna moved.

3. Their home sold.

Just for Fun
Building a Tree

Add as many modifers as you can to the following sentence to make a big diagram tree!

cow | jumped

Chapter Review

Choose words from the list below to complete each of the following sentences:
vertical line, slanting line, subject, verb, adjective, adverb, modifiers, possessive pronoun, prepositional phrase.

1. Either a noun or a pronoun may be used as the _____ of a sentence.

2. The predicate always begins with a _____.

3. Adjectives, adverbs, possessive nouns, and prepositional phrases are all _____.

4. A word that modifies the subject is an _____.

5. A word that modifies the verb is an _____.

6. You can diagram an adjective by placing it on a _____ _____ under the noun.

7. The subject and the predicate are separated by a _____ _____ that goes through the horizontal line.

8. _____ _____ may be used as adjectives or as adverbs.

Time to Write

Describe how to get to the nearest library from your house, and include several landmarks such as "the large red-and-white sign," etc.

CHAPTER THREE
DIRECT OBJECTS and INDIRECT OBJECTS

Direct Objects

Active verbs such as "throw," "break," "send," and others carry the action from the noun subject to a noun or pronoun called the *direct object*. We diagram direct objects by placing them after the verb with a short vertical line separating them from the verb.

Example: Barbara broke the *vase*.

In this sentence, "vase" is the direct object. The action of breaking carried from the subject to the direct object.

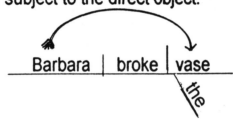

Let's look at another example:

Example: Bryan made a *sandwich*.

The subject "Bryan" did the making, and "sandwich" is the direct object of his action.

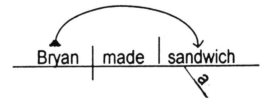

Practice Diagramming Direct Objects

Diagram the sentences below. First find the subject and predicate, and then locate the direct object.

1. April saw the hunters.

2. She watched them through her window.

3. The hunters tracked a deer.

4. The deer heard the hunters.

5. The hunters missed the deer.

Pronouns Used as Direct Objects

A pronoun may take the place of a noun being used as an object. It may have a different form than when it is used as a subject.

SUBJECTS
I, we,
you, you
they, he, she, it

OBJECTS
me, us
you, you
them, him, her, it

> **Example:** Jerry invited *me*.

$$\underline{\quad \text{Jerry} \mid \text{invited} \mid \text{me} \quad}$$

Diagram each of the following sentences:

1. Kent waved it.

2. Angela saw him.

3. I like her.

4. We invited him.

5. I found it.

28

Indirect Objects

Sentences that have direct objects may also have *indirect objects*. An indirect object may have an unspoken "to" before it.

Example: I gave *Barbara* a bracelet.

"Bracelet" is the direct object in this sentence. The action of the subject "I" carries over to the noun object "bracelet." The noun "Barbara" is an indirect object.

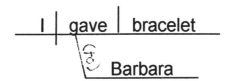

Example: I asked the *repairman* a simple question.

"Repairman" is the indirect object. "Question" is the direct object.

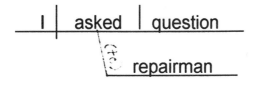

Practice Diagramming Indirect Objects

Diagram the sentences below, placing indirect objects beneath the verb.

1. Andy gave the campers information.

2. The campers told him "Thank you."

3. The ranger gave Andy a radio.

4. Andy gave the campers directions to the shelter.

5. The campers wrote him a note.

Just for Fun

Who uses these tools?

Guess the job of the person who uses each of the following tools:

Tool	Job
1. spatula, skillet	_____
2. wrench, screwdriver	_____
3. lasso, chaps	_____
4. map, telephone	_____
5. helmet, tool belt	_____

Chapter Review

Circle the direct object in each of the following sentences.

1. Bryan frightened the fish.

2. The fish splashed Bryan.

3. Bryan grabbed its fin.

4. The fin stuck Bryan.

Complete each of the following sentences by selecting the correct word or words to fill the blank.

1. A verb must be _____ to take a direct object.
    (active, in a state of being)

2. A direct object is always a _____.
    (noun or pronoun, preposition)

Circle the indirect object in each of the following sentences.

1. Erica gave us her promise.

2. She told us her secret.

Complete the following sentences.

1. A sentence can have an indirect object only if it has a _____ object.

2. An indirect object may have an unexpressed word--_____.

Time to Write

Tools are an important part of any civilization. What tools are most important to people today? What tools will be needed in the future? Invent a tool that you think will be used 100 years from now, and write a paragraph about it.

_____

_____

_____

_____

_____

_____

_____

CHAPTER FOUR
PREDICATE NOUNS, PRONOUNS, AND ADJECTIVES

Some verbs do not show action. Verbs such as **is, are, was, were, am, be, looks, smells, feels, and tastes** show a state of being. They are called *intransitive* verbs. "Intransitive" means that there is no "carry over" of action between the subject and the noun following the verb, and there can be no direct object .

The following example shows an *intransitive* verb that is *complete*; that is, there is no need for another word on the baseline with the subject and verb.

Example: Margaret *is* here.

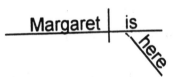

When intransitive verbs connect a subject with a noun or pronoun or adjective following the verb, the verbs are called *intransitive "linking"* verbs. In this example, the verb connects the subject "Kenney" with the noun "friend."

Example: Kenney *is* my friend.

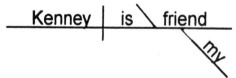

The noun "friend" has much the same meaning as the subject "Kenney." The second noun is called a **predicate noun.** (A pronoun may substitute for the noun and would be called a **predicate pronoun**.)

Diagramming Predicate Nouns and Predicate Pronouns

We diagram predicate nouns and pronouns by placing a short slanting line between the verb and the predicate noun. The slanting line points back toward the subject.

Example: Erica was the team *captain*.

"Was" is a linking verb connecting the subject "Erica" with the predicate noun "captain." "Erica" and "captain" are the same person.

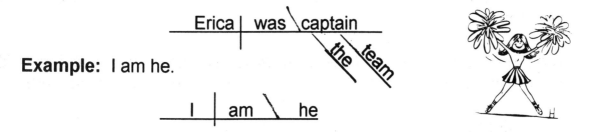

Example: I am he.

"Am" is a linking verb connecting the subject "I" with the predicate pronoun "he." "I" and "he" are the same person.

Diagram the following sentences. Remember to place a short slanted line between the verb and the predicate noun or pronoun.

1. Arthur was the hero of the play.

2. The play was a documentary.

Subjective and Objective Forms

One of the reasons for diagramming sentences is to be able to understand what is correct. When a pronoun is used as the subject, it must be in *subjective* form such as "who," "he," or "she." (See pronoun list p. 28.)

Example: *She* spotted her prey.

"She" is a pronoun used as the subject and is in subjective form.

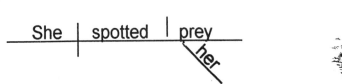

A pronoun used as the object of a verb (or the object of a preposition) must be in *objective* form such as "whom," "him," or "her."

Example: Amy visited *him*.

"Him" is the object of the active verb "visited." It receives the action of the subject "Amy."

Amy | visited | him

When a pronoun follows a linking verb, it is used as a predicate pronoun, and it must be in *subjective* form because it is equal to the subject.

Example: Jason is *he*.

"He" is a predicate pronoun in subjective form following the linking verb "is."

Jason | is ＼ he

Practice Diagramming Subjective and Objective Forms

Select the correct form for each of the sentences below, and then diagram the sentence.

1. Jacob called (she, her).

2. (She, Her) screamed!

3. (They, Them) were her heroes!

4. I love (you, you)!

5. Jacob teased (she, her).

Using Who and Whom *

Diagramming can make the use of "who" and "whom" a simple task. We just need to remember that "who" is the subjective form (It can be used as a subject) and "whom" is the objective form.

Questions such as "Who are you?" are usually diagrammed as statements; that is, the subject is "you," and the predicate pronoun is "who."

Example: Who are you?

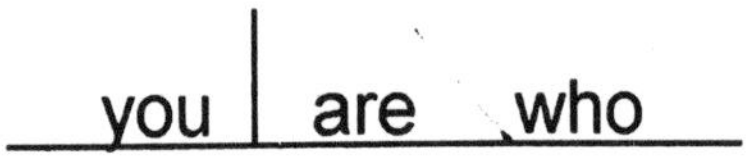

```
   you | are \ who
```

You can see from the diagram that the object form "whom" would not fit in this sentence because "are" is a linking verb, and the pronoun following "are" must be in subjective form.

Example: Whom did you visit?

```
   you | did visit | whom
```

This diagram shows "whom" as the direct object of the verb "did visit." "Whom" is the objective form of "who." If the sentence were reworded, it might say, "Did you visit *her*? (objective) or Did you visit *him*? (objective).

---

* Use of the pronouns "I" and "me" might also be considered here. "I" is subjective, and "me" is objective. For exercises, please see the Supplementary Exercises in the back of the book.

Predicate Adjectives

Linking verbs may be followed by an adjective rather than a noun or pronoun. The adjective describes the noun subject. Such adjectives are called *predicate adjectives*. Predicate adjectives are diagrammed just like predicate nouns.

Example: Allen was *shy.*

The verb "was" is a linking verb, and the adjective "shy" describes the noun subject "Allen." "Shy" is a predicate adjective.

$$\text{Allen} \mid \text{was} \diagdown \text{shy}$$

Example: We were *tired.*

The verb "were" is a linking verb, and the adjective "tired" describes the pronoun subject "We." "Tired" is a predicate adjective.

$$\text{We} \mid \text{were} \diagdown \text{tired}$$

Practice diagramming predicate adjectives.

1. James feels sick.

2. Alicia will be excited.

Practice Diagramming Predicate Nouns, Pronouns, and Adjectives

Diagram the sentences below.

1. Frank felt sleepy.

2. Rosemary was awake.

3. The cake tastes delicious!

4. The steps are steep.

5. I am being careful.

6. George was the king.

7. Who are you?

8. April is the best month.

Just for Fun

Name this character!

Make up a name and an identity for each of the characters below. Include information such as how old the character is, what the person does for a living, what he/she likes to do during free time, and where he/she lives. Have fun!

Chapter Review

Diagram each of the following sentences. HINT: Look at the verb first, and decide whether it is an action verb or an intransitive verb. Some sentences may contain direct objects. (A list of intransitive verbs is on p. 34.)

1. Laura is the manager.

2. She opened the shop yesterday.

3. Business is booming!

4. Laura is excited about her job.

Select the correct answer, and diagram the sentence.

1. _____ will enter the race?
   (Who, Whom)

2. _____ did you choose?
   (Who, Whom)

Time to Write

How well do you know yourself? Can you describe yourself so that anyone would be able to pick you out of a group of people? How tall are you? What kinds of clothes do you usually wear? What kinds of things are you usually doing?

Write a short description in the space below.

_____

_____

_____

_____

_____

_____

_____

_____

_____

CHAPTER FIVE
COMPOUND CONSTRUCTIONS

Compound Modifiers

Two or more words, phrases, or sentences joined by a coordinating conjunction (**and**, **but**, or **or**) form *compound* constructions. Adjectives, adverbs, and prepositional phrases become compound modifiers when they are joined by coordinating conjunctions.

Example: Myra was *excited and happy.*

In this sentence, the two adjectives "excited" and "happy" form a compound predicate adjective.

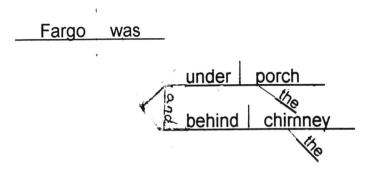

Example: Fargo was *under the porch and behind the chimney.*

The prepositional phrases "under the porch" and "behind the chimney" are used as adverbs modifying "was" and telling where Fargo was.

Practice Diagramming Modifiers

Diagram the sentences below.

1. George felt fearful and nauseous.

2. Matt was confident and excited.

3. George hid between the refrigerator and the pantry.

4. Matt searched near and far.

5. George was well hidden and very quiet.

Compound Subjects

How are these two sentences different?

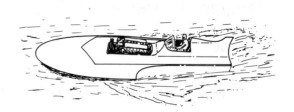

Joey captured the boat.

Joey and Nick captured the boat.

The second sentence has a *compound subject*. When two or more nouns or pronouns are used as the subject, we say that we have a compound subject. Compound subjects are diagrammed on parallel lines with the conjunction on a line between them.

Example: Joey and Nick captured the boat.

Joey / Nick — and — | captured | boat

Let's look at another example:

Example: Skiing and swimming are fun.

The compound subject is "skiing and swimming."

Skiing / swimming — and — | are \ fun

Practice Diagramming Compound Subjects

Diagram the sentences below.

1. Chuck and Marti shared a soda.

2. Sodas and cones sell well.

3. The owner and the manager are the same person.

4. Gary and Anita work at the soda shop.

5. Gary and the owner invented jelly bean ice cream.

Compound Predicates

When two or more verbs are used as the predicate, we say that we have a *compound predicate*.

A compound predicate is diagrammed much like a compound subject except that the construction is on the right side of the diagram.

Example: Teresa *screamed and giggled*.

"Teresa" is the subject, and "screamed" and "giggled" is the compound predicate.

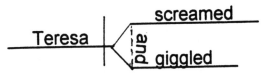

Exercise: Diagram the following sentence.

The alligator snapped and snarled.

Practice Diagramming

Diagram the sentences below.

1. Daniel Boone and Davy Crockett were pioneers.

2. They hunted and trapped.

3. The cap was coonskin or squirrelskin.

4. They slept under the moon and the stars.

5. The Indians and the pioneers hunted.

Compound Sentences

Up to now, we have studied *simple sentences*; that is, sentences that have only one subject (or a compound subject) and only one predicate (or a compound predicate). The subject-predicate combination is called a *clause*. A simple sentence has only one clause.

Example: Jerry ran to the house.

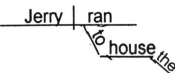

We can make our writing more interesting by combining thoughts into sentences that have more than one subject and predicate combination. One way to do this is to combine two or more sentences together into a *compound sentence.*

A compound sentence has two or more *clauses* joined together by one or more coordinating conjunctions. Notice that a comma comes before the coordinating conjunction.

Example: Linda fell from the horse, *and* Jerry ran to the house, but no one could help him.

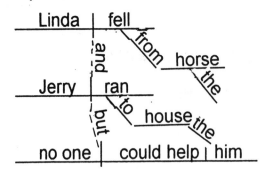

Practice Diagramming Compound Sentences

Diagram the sentences below. Place each clause on a separate line.

1. Ripley tugged and tugged, but the bone stayed in the ground.

2. He growled, and he barked, and he showed his teeth, but nothing worked for him.

3. Then Lulu came, and Ripley forgot the bone.

More Practice!

Diagram the following sentences. Watch out! Some of these are tricky!

1. Jerry and Wanda visited the mountains and the seashore, and Wanda took hundreds of pictures.

2. A cactus grows in the desert, but it will not grow near the ocean.

3. Wanda saw a sea lion and a walrus, and she was fascinated by them.

4. Wanda smiled and chattered about the sea animals.

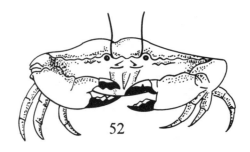

Just for Fun

Playing Detective

Follow the clues below to discover what Mr. Snoop is looking for.

1. Last letter of the word that describes an animal that may live at your house.

    — — — —

2. Last two letters of the word that tells where wild animals may live safely in a large city.

    — — — —

3. First letter of a word that describes a drink that English people enjoy.

    — — — —

4. Abbreviation for a halfback football player.

    — —

5. All of the letters for a word that describes what people do when they are in a hurry! They __ __ __ __!

Mr. Snoop is looking for his __ __ __ __ __ __ __ __ __ __.

Chapter Review

Complete the following sentences.

1. The conjunctions _____, _____, and _____ are common coordinating conjunctions.

2. Coordinating conjunctions may be used to join two adjectives, adverbs, or prepositional phrases to form a _____ modifier.

3. Coordinating conjunctions can also be used to form compound sentences. A compound sentence has two or more

   _____ .

Circle the compound subjects, predicates, and modifiers in the following sentences.

1. Manuel worked long and hard.

2. He stooped under the wagon and climbed over the sick mule.

3. The mule and the wagon seemed hopelessly entangled.

4. Manuel used his brain and brawn.

5. The wagon and the mule survived the upset.

Circle the clauses in each of the following compound sentences.

1. Jeff's mother bought a ticket, and she went to the play.

2. Jeff spotted her in the audience, and he invited her backstage.

Time to Write

Give directions to your home to someone who is not familiar with the area. First list the directions, one step at a time. Then write the same directions in paragraph form, combining some of the sentences by using the coordinating conjunctions **and**, **but**, or **or**.

CHAPTER SIX
COMPLEX SENTENCES

In the last chapter, we combined two clauses of *equal* value together to form *compound sentences*. In this chapter, we shall see how clauses of *unequal* value may be used together to form *complex sentences*.

Complex sentences have a main clause, usually called the *independent clause*, and one or more *dependent clauses*. The main clause makes sense all by itself. The dependent clause is like a helper. It adds to the meaning of the main clause, but it can't do the job by itself.

A dependent clause may be used as a noun, an adjective, or an adverb.

Noun Clause

A noun clause identifies a person, place, or thing just as a noun does. It may be used any place that a noun would be used.

Example: *"A stitch in time saves nine"* still makes sense.

The noun clause "A stitch in time saves nine" is the subject of the sentence.

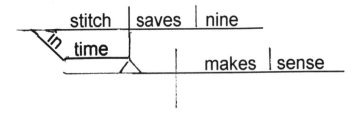

Noun Clause (Continued)

Example: The baby wanted *whatever his older brother had.*

"Whatever his older brother had" is a noun clause used as the object of the verb "wanted."

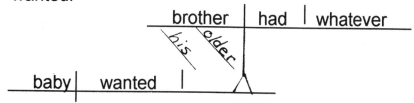

Example: She reached for *what he was holding.*

"What he was holding" is a noun clause used as the object of the preposition "for."

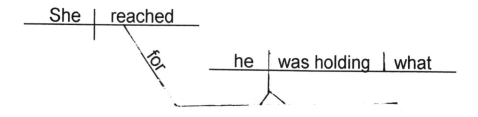

Practice Diagramming Noun Clauses

Diagram each of the following sentences. First, find the independent clause, and then locate the dependent clause and decide how it is being used.

1. Whoever wins the contest will receive the trophy.

2. I am who I am.

3. That I could win did not seem possible.

4. I saw that he was very strong.

5. No one expected that he would faint.

More Practice with Noun Clauses

In each of the following sentences, circle the noun clause (or clauses), and tell how it is used.

1. Whatever Maggie wanted was what Arthur wanted. (2)

2. Maggie wanted what she could not have.

3. What she could not have was a vacation in Ireland.

4. Maggie knew that war had broken out in Ireland.

5. She knew that travel would be impossible.

Adjective Clauses

An adjective clause may be used in place of an adjective.

Adjective clauses are often introduced by "that," "which," or "who." (Noun clauses may also be introduced by "that," "which," or "who.") How the clause is used is what determines whether it is a noun or an adjective clause.

Example: The land *that my brother owns* has lakes on it.

In this sentence, "that my brother owns" tells which land. The clause is being used as an adjective.

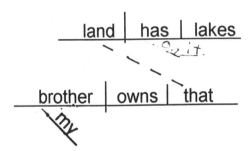

Example: He caught a fish *that was thirty inches long.*

The clause "that was thirty inches long" is an adjective clause modifying "fish."

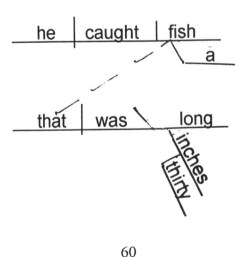

More about Adjective Clauses

Adjective clauses that limit the noun they modify are called *restrictive* clauses and do not require any punctuation.

Example: I saw the car *that my grandfather loved*.

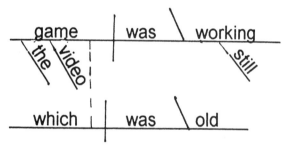

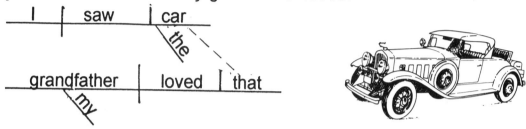

The adjective clause "that my grandfather loved" describes a specific car. It limits the word "car."

Adjective clauses that do not limit but merely add information are called *nonrestrictive* clauses. They are set off by commas in the sentence.

Example: The video game, *which was old*, was still working.

Find the adjective clause in each sentence below, and determine whether or not it needs to be set off by commas. Add commas where needed. Then diagram the sentences.

1. The lamp which was lit was brass with a glass top.

2. I saw the bedroom that the boys used.

3. The lady who gave the tour had a monotone voice.

Adverb Clauses

An adverb clause may be used to modify a verb, an adjective, or another adverb, just as an adverb does .Adverb clauses are often introduced by "because", "since", "as if", and "as though."

Example: She danced *as though she were inspired by heaven.**

In this sentence, the independent clause is "she danced." The dependent clause is introduced by "as though." It is an adverb clause telling how she danced.

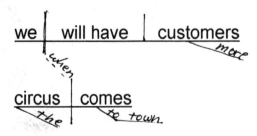

She | danced

as though

she | were inspired

by heaven

*You may have noticed that the subject "she" is singular, and the verb "were" is plural. Subject-verb agreement is sometimes purposely reversed when the topic is clearly an extraordinary situation. Example: "If I were king . . . "

Adverb clauses often begin a sentence by placing a condition on an action.

Example: *When the circus comes to town*, we will have more customers!

The adverb clause "When the circus comes to town" modifies the verb   "will have." The action (having more customers) depends upon the   condition (the circus comes to town).

we | will have | customers

more

...when

circus | comes

the   to town

Practice Diagramming Adverb Clauses

Diagram the following sentences. Remember to draw a line between the adverb clause and the word it modifies.

1. Arlene was disappointed because her new car did not have air conditioning.

2. Since she lived in Arizona, she would use air conditioning for several months.

3. Because Snappy Motors had a good reputation, she went to them for service.

4. Arlene is happy now because she is cool.

More Practice with Adverb Clauses

When an adverb clause begins a sentence or comes before the main thought, we insert a comma between the adverb clause and the independent clause. When an adverb clause follows the main thought, no comma is needed.

Example:
Because Forrest believed in himself, he became successful.
Forrest became successful because he believed in himself.

Develop adverb clauses to combine the statements below. Punctuate them correctly.

1. Bill Cosby wanted better programming. He began a new show.

_____

_____

_____

2. He was tired of violence. He made NBC an offer.

_____

_____

_____

Just for Fun

ADD-A-CLAUSE--How many clauses can you add to the sentence below and still have it make sense? You may add noun clauses, adjective clauses, or adverb clauses!

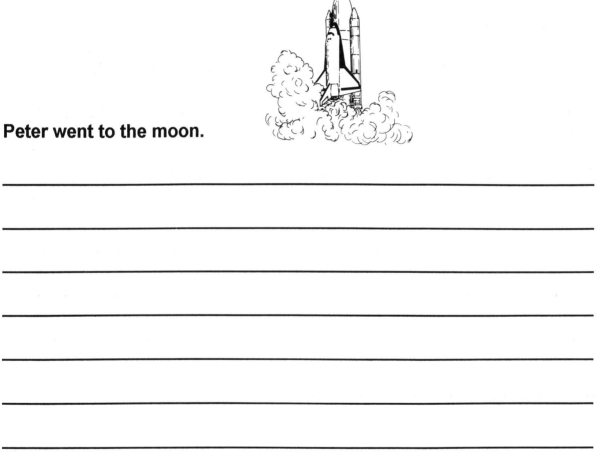

Peter went to the moon.

_____

_____

_____

_____

_____

_____

Chapter Review

Diagram each of the following sentences.

1. Allen looked at the boat, which had seen better days.

2. The boat that was still seaworthy was gone.

3. The old hull, which was cracked, leaked water.

4. The engine that ran was rusty on the outside.

5. Since Allen had the bucket of tar, he repaired the leaks.

Time to Write

Do you ever daydream? If you could be anyplace in the world, where would you go? Describe the spot of your dreams!

_____

_____

_____

_____

_____

_____

_____

_____

_____

_____

CHAPTER SEVEN--VERBALS--
PARTICIPLES, GERUNDS, AND
INFINITIVES

Verbals are interesting parts of our language because they are all combinations of a verb and another part of speech. They are a little like an ice cream sundae--part ice cream and part syrup!

Participles

Participles are a verb form used as an adjective. Participles can modify a noun and can be modified by an adverb.

Example: The substitute quarterback is *playing*.

"Playing" is a form of the verb "play." In this sentence, the participle is used as a predicate adjective.

$$\underline{\text{quarterback} \mid \text{is} \diagdown \text{playing}}$$

Example: Jeff, *running the vacuum cleaner*, did not hear the phone.

The phrase "running the vacuum cleaner" is a participial phrase beginning with the participle "running." The noun "cleaner" is the object of the participle "running."

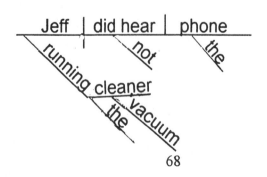

Participles (continued)

Example: The deer, *hidden by a tree*, was not seen.

The phrase "hidden by a tree" is a participal phrase beginning with the participle "hidden." "By a tree" is a prepositional phrase used as an adverb to modify the participle "hidden."

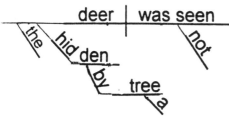

Example: Mark, *having already seen the movie*, declined the invitation.

The past perfect participle "having seen" begins the phrase. "Already" is an adverb modifying "having seen," and "movie" is the object of "having seen."

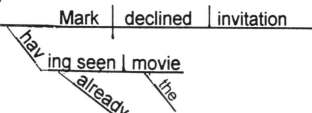

Example of Common Verb Forms

Present Tense	Past Tense	Past Participle
arise	arose	arisen
begin	began	begun
catch	caught	caught
do	did	done

Practice Diagramming Participles

Diagram the sentences below. Remember that participles will modify nouns.

1. Harrison, running from a large dog, tripped over a log.

2. The dog, excited by the chase, drooled on Harrison.

3. Harrison, having already had a shower, pushed the dog away.

4. The dog, thrilled at the attention, licked Harrison's face.

5. Harrison, drenched in doggy saliva, crawled to a tree.

Gerunds

Gerunds are verb forms that end in -ing and are used as nouns. Because nouns can be subjects or objects in a sentence, gerunds may also be subjects or objects. Like a verb, a gerund may also be followed by an object.

Example: *Swimming* is my favorite sport.

"Swimming" is a gerund used as the subject of the sentence.

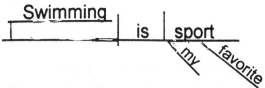

Example: Ted enjoys *playing* tennis.

"Playing" is a gerund that takes the noun "tennis" as its object. The entire phrase "playing tennis" is the object of the verb "enjoys."
The diagram shows the gerund phrase on a tiny pedestal to show that the whole phrase and not just the gerund is the object of the verb "enjoys."

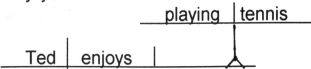

Practice Diagramming Gerunds

Diagram the sentences below. Remember to place gerund phrases on a small pedestal.

1. I like traveling.

2. I like meeting new people.

3. Posing for pictures is fun

4. Eating exotic foods can be scary!

5. Coming home always feels good.

Infinitives

An infinitive is made up of the word "to" plus a verb--"to explain," "to grow."
An infinitive can take an object, and it may be used as a noun or as an
adjective or as an adverb.

Infinitives are diagrammed much as gerunds are. When the infinitive phrase
is used as the subject or object of a sentence, the phrase is placed upon a
small pedestal.

Example: His dream was *to win*.

"To win" is an infinitive used as the predicate noun of the sentence.

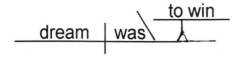

Example: *To reach the top* took determination.

The infinitive phrase "to reach the top" is the subject of the sentence.
"Top" is the object of "to reach."

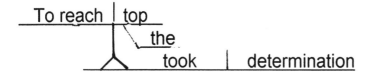

73

Practice Diagramming Infinitives

Complete each of the following sentences with your own infinitive or infinitive phrase. Then diagram each sentence.

1. I know how _____.

2. I like _____.

3. _____ would be fun.

4. I wanted _____ an astronaut.

5. My dad asked me _____ what I was feeling.

Just for Fun

Exotic Places

Fill each blank with the name of the country that matches the city listed beside it.

1. London, _____

2. Paris, _____

3. Brussels, _____

4. Rio de Janerio, _____

5. Rome, _____

6. Toronto, _____

7. Moscow, _____

8. Hong Kong, _____

9. Oslo, _____

10. Cairo, _____

Chapter Review

1. Participles, gerunds, and infinitives are all _____ forms.

2. How do verbals act like verbs?

   _____

   _____

   _____

3. Participles are verb/_____ parts of speech. They modify
   _____.

4. Gerunds usually end in _____. They are used as
   _____.

5. Infinitives are the word "_____" plus a verb. Infinitives may be used
   as _____, _____, or
   _____.

Circle the verbals in the following sentence. You need not label them.

   I love to listen to the sound of my skis gliding across the snow.

Time to Write

The Ideal Friend

Are you a good friend? What do you think is the most important quality in a friend? Write a paragraph describing your idea of an ideal friend.

CHAPTER EIGHT--SPECIAL CASES

Appositives

A noun placed near another noun that has the same meaning is called a *noun in apposition* or an *appositive*.

Example: My son *Juan* loves model airplanes.
Also: Juan, my *son*, loves model airplanes.

Notice that in the first sentence the two words "son" and "Juan" are next to each other and "son" helps to identify "Juan." In this case, the two words may be placed together on the diagram.

In the second sentence, the word "son" is not really needed for the sentence to make sense. When a word or phrase like "my son" is included but is not important to the sentence structure, we say that the phrase is *parenthetical*. We can show it on the diagram within parentheses.

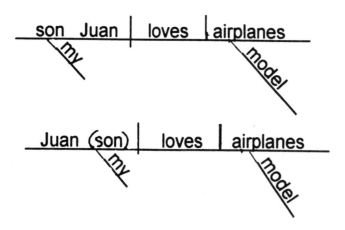

Noun of Direct Address

A person being spoken to is often called to attention by using his name.

Example: *Jacque*, play something for me!

A name used in this way is referred to as a *noun of direct address*. It is not really part of the sentence structure, and it may be left out of the diagram or may be set beside the diagram on a separate line.

The subject of the example sentence is an unexpressed "you" and should be included in the diagram in parentheses.

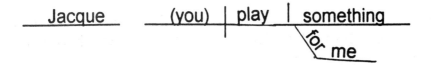

Example: *Mary*, aren't you enjoying his music?

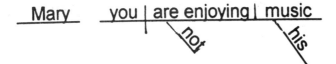

Practice Diagramming Special Cases

Diagram each of the following sentences.

1. Mr. Botsworth, my employer, said he would loan me the money for a new ferret cage.

2. His wife Hannah agreed with him.

3. David, I have good news for you!

4. Brownie, sit!

5. My ferret Brownie is not trained.

Just for Fun

Create a Story . . .

Write a simple story plot using the characters pictured here.

_____

_____

_____

_____

_____

_____

Chapter Review

Complete the following sentences.

1. A noun in apposition has the same meaning as another _____ that is near it in the sentence.

2. A _____ sits next to the noun that means the same in a diagram of the sentence.

3. A noun of direct address does _____ have an actual place in the sentence structure.

4. The subject in a sentence using a noun of direct address is often an unexpressed _____.

5. When an unexpressed "you" is the subject of a sentence, it is placed in the diagram in _____.

Time to Write

Suppose that you are a modern pioneer moving to a new land. You bring modern equipment with you, but there are no laws governing the people. What is the first law you would suggest, and why?

Supplementary Exercises

Additions to p. 38

I and Me

"I" is the subjective form, and "me" is the objective form. Which form would you use in each of the following cases?   If you are not sure of what to use, diagram the sentence.   (Answers at the bottom of page.)

1. _____ began my project yesterday.

2. The grocer gave _____ boxes for it.

3. My brother and _____ carried the boxes from the store.

4. My mother said that my brother and _____ could use the garage for our project.

5. My dad cleared a spot for my brother and _____ .

Answers: 1. I , 2. me , 3. I, 4. I, 5. me.

Diagramming Answers

pp. 2-7 (Suggestions. Answers will vary)
   boots, smiled, They, tall, mournfully, off, near, and, when, look

p. 8 (Suggestions. Answers will vary.)
   1. John 2. He 3. on 4. barn 5. old 6. house 7. very 8. and 9. John 10. Wow! 11. John 12. It

p. 9 1. Washington 2. Lincoln 3. Coolidge 4. Roosevelts, Theodore, Franklin 5. Carter

p. 10 1. h 2. g. 3. I 4. d 5. e 6. c 7. b 8. a

p. 14. 1. The | lion | growled   2. Robby | shivered   3. Sarah | cried

   4. The | dog | whimpered   5. The | movie | ended

p. 15. 1. dog | barked   2. light | shone   3. boy | played   4. wind | blew   5. he | shouted

p. 17. 1. The big | bug | hummed   2. The tall dark | man | sang   3. The silly old | hen | clucked

   4. The green | parakeet | chirped   5. Harold | listened

p. 19. 1. Tina | skated gracefully   2. The brand new | skates | shone   3. She | turned sharply very

   4. The | skates | squealed loudly   5. The very beautiful | skater | bowed

p. 21. 1. Mark | looked into the barrel   2. The | barrel | smelled like pinecones   3. A | squirrel | watched from a nearby tree

   4. He | watched from his perch very closely   5. Mark | grinned at the squirrel

p. 22 1. Her | mother | called   2. It's | antenna | moved   3. Their | home | sold

Answers Continued)

p. 24 1. subject   2. verb   3. modifiers   4. adjective   5. adverb   6. slanting line
7. vertical line   8. prepositional phrase

p. 27 1. April | saw | hunters (the)

2. She | watched | them (through her window)

3. hunters | tracked | deer (The) (a)

4. deer | heard | hunters (The) (the)

5. hunters | missed | deer (The) (the)

p.28. 1. Kent | waved | it

2. Angela | saw | him

3. I | like | her

4. We | invited | him

5. I | found | it

p. 30. 1. Andy | gave | information (to) campers (the)

2. campers | told | "Thank you" (The) (to) him

3. ranger | gave | radio (The) (to) Andy

4. Andy | gave | directions (to) campers (the) to shelter (the)

5. campers | wrote | note (The) (to) him (a)

p. 31. 1. chef   2. mechanic   3. cowboy   4. travel agent   5. telephone repairman

p. 32. 1. fish   2. Bryan   3. fin   4. Bryan   1. active   2. noun or pronoun
1. us   2. us   1. direct   2. to

p. 35. 1. Arthur | was | hero (the) (of play) (the)

2. play | was \ documentary (The) (a)

p. 37. 1. her   Jacob | called | her

2. She   She | screamed

Answers (Continued)

p. 37 (Continued)

3. They   They | were \ heroes
                          \ her

4. You   I | love | you

5. her   Jacob | teased | her

p. 39   1.   James | feels | sick

2.   Alicia | will be \ excited

p. 40   1.   Frank | felt \ sleepy

2.   Rosemary | was \ awake

3.   cake | tastes \ delicious
              \ The

4.   steps | are \ steep
            \ The

5.   I | am being \ careful

6.   George | was \ king
                    \ the

7.   you | are \ who

8.   April | is \ month
              \ the \ best

p. 42.   1.   Laura | is \ manager
                      \ the

2.   She | opened | shop
        \ yesterday \ the

3.   Business | is \ booming

4.   Laura | is \ excited
              \ about \ job \ her

1.   Who | will enter | race
                      \ the

2.   you | did choose | whom

p. 45   1.   George | felt \ fearful
                       and
                       nauseous

2.   Matt | was \ confident
                 and
                 exited

3.   George | hid
        between \ and \ refrigerator \ the
                     \ pantry \ the

4.   Matt | searched
              \ near
               and
               far

5.   George | was \ hidden \ well
                   and
                   quiet \ very

p. 47.   1.   Chuck
              and \ shared | soda \ a
          Marti

2.   Sodas
        and \ | sell \ well
     cones

Answers (Continued)

p. 47 (Continued)

3.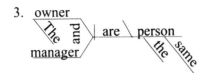

4.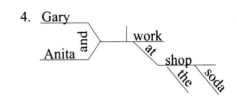

5.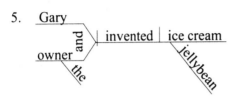

p. 48.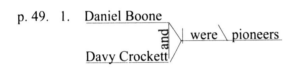

p. 49. 1.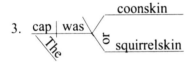

2.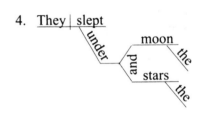

3.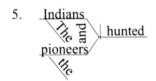

4.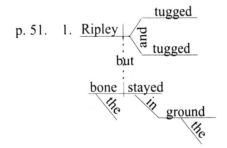

5.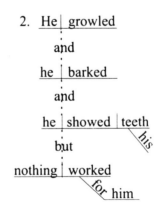

p. 51. 1.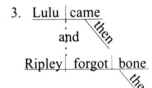

2.

3.

Answers (Continued)

p. 52. 1.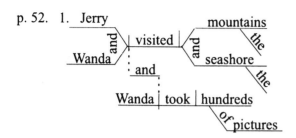

2.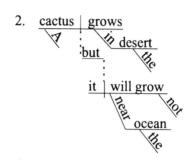

3.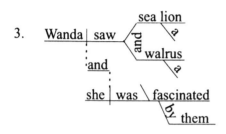

4.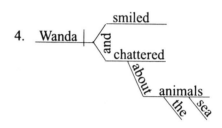

p. 53. 1. cat 2. zoo 3. tea 4. h b 5. rush 6. toothbrush

p. 54. 1. and, or, but   2. compound   3. clauses
1. long and hard   2. stooped and climbed   3. mule and wagon   4. brain and brawn
5. wagon and mule
1. Jeff's mother bought a ticket. She went to the play.   2. Jeff spotted her in the audience. He invited her backstage.

p. 58. 1.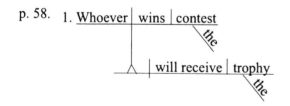

2.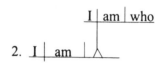

Note: There may be other ways to diagram this sentence

3. That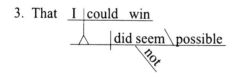

Note: "That" is an introductory word and may be set aside on a separate line. "Seems" is considered to be intransitive just as the words "feels", "smells", and "tastes" are.

4.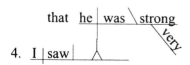

5. No one | expected

Answers (Continued)

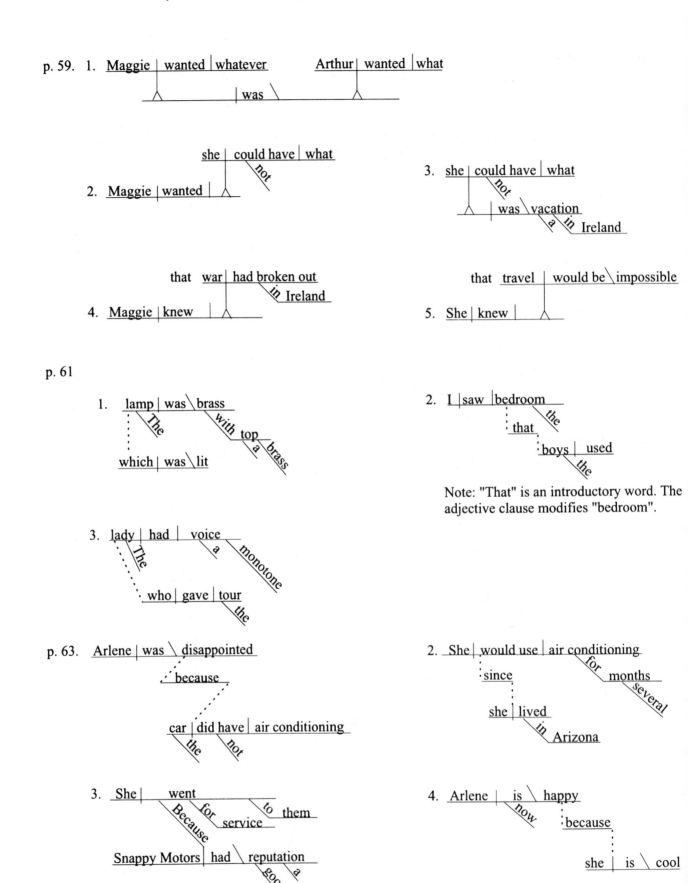

p. 59. 1. Maggie | wanted | whatever   Arthur | wanted | what
                                       | was \

2. Maggie | wanted |
        she | could have | what
                  \ not

3. she | could have | what
              \ not
        | was \ vacation
              a \ in \ Ireland

4. Maggie | knew |
        that war | had broken out
                  in Ireland

5. She | knew |
        that travel | would be \ impossible

p. 61

1. lamp | was \ brass
    The
        with \ top
             a \ brass
    which | was \ lit

2. I | saw | bedroom
        that the
              boys | used
                   the

Note: "That" is an introductory word. The adjective clause modifies "bedroom".

3. lady | had | voice
    The   a \ monotone
    who | gave | tour
               the

p. 63. Arlene | was \ disappointed
            because
        car | did have | air conditioning
        the   not

2. She | would use | air conditioning
        since   for \ months
                          several
        she | lived
            in \ Arizona

3. She | went
        Because for \ to \ them
                service
        Snappy Motors | had \ reputation
                           good \ a

4. Arlene | is \ happy
            now
                because
        she | is \ cool

Answers (Continued)

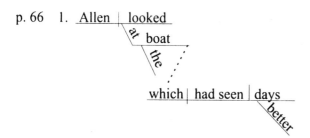

p. 66   1. Allen | looked
at boat
the
which | had seen | days
better

2. boat | was \ gone
The
that | was \ seaworthy
still

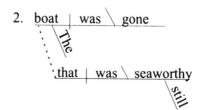

3. hull | leaked | water
old The
which | was \ cracked

4. engine | was \ rusty
The
on outside
the
that | ran

5. he | repaired | leaks
the
since
Allen | had | bucket
of tar the

p. 70.   1. Harrison | tripped
running over log
from a
dog
large a

2. dog | drooled
The on Harrison
excited
by chase
the

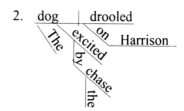

3. Harrison | pushed | dog
away the
having had | shower
already a

4. dog | licked | face
The thrilled Harrison's
at attention
the

5. Harrison | crawled
to tree
drenched a
in saliva
doggy

Answers (Continued)

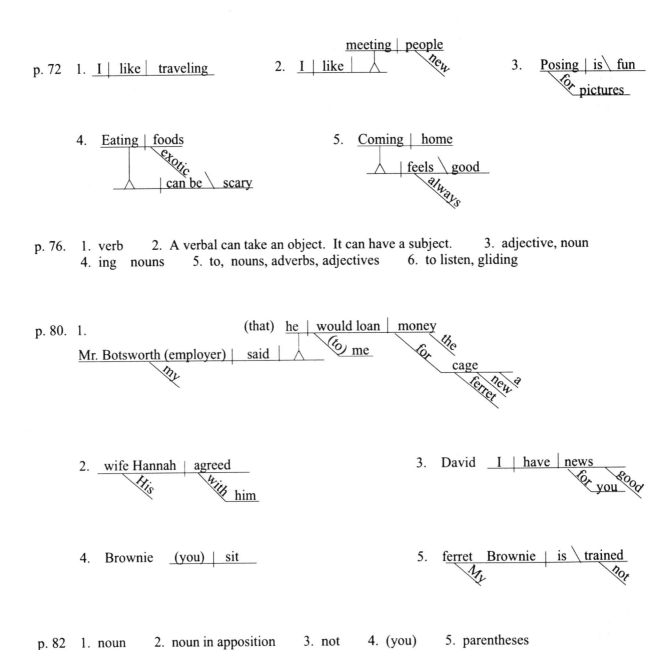

p. 72   1.   I | like | traveling

2.   I | like | meeting | people
                         new

3.   Posing | is \ fun
              for pictures

4.   Eating | foods
              exotic
         | can be \ scary

5.   Coming | home
         | feels \ good
              always

p. 76.   1. verb   2. A verbal can take an object. It can have a subject.   3. adjective, noun
         4. ing   nouns   5. to, nouns, adverbs, adjectives   6. to listen, gliding

p. 80.   1.

Mr. Botsworth (employer) | said | (that) he | would loan | money
         my   (to) me   for the
                                                   cage
                                                   ferret new a

2.   wife Hannah | agreed
         His   with him

3.   David   I | have | news
                        for you good

4.   Brownie   (you) | sit

5.   ferret Brownie | is \ trained
         My   not

p. 82   1. noun   2. noun in apposition   3. not   4. (you)   5. parentheses